Self Epiphany Esteem & Confidence Workbook

Workbook

Discover Your Purpose & Live Empowered

Chizoma C. Nosiri, Ph.D.

IRISON BOOKS & PUBLICATIONS

Maryland • Irisonbp.com

Published by Irison, LLC (Irison Books & Publications) www.irisonbp.com

Copyright © 2019 Irison, LLC (Irison Books & Publications)

All rights are reserved. No part of this book may be reproduced, stored in a retrieval system or transmitted in any form or by any means, electronic, mechanical, photocopying, recording, including information storage and retrieval systems, without written permission from the publisher: Irison, LLC (Irison Books & Publications).

Permissions: For information on how to request permissions to reproduce any part of this book, please visit www.irisonbp.com.

Advertising: Advertising, inserts and artwork enquiries should be addressed to Irison, LLC, please visit www.irisonbp.com.

The author of this book does not dispense medical advice or prescribe the use of any technique as a form of treatment for physical, emotional, or medical problems without the advice of a physician, either directly or indirectly. The intent of the author is only to offer information of a general nature to help the reader in their quest for emotional and spiritual well-being. In the event you use any of the information in this book for yourself, the author and the publisher, assume no responsibility for your actions.

Disclaimer: Statements of fact and opinion in the pages of this book are those of the respective authors and contributors and not of Irison, LLC. Irison, LLC does not make any representation, express or implied, in respect of the accuracy of the material in this book and cannot accept any legal responsibility or liability for any errors or omissions that may be made. The reader should make his/her own evaluation as to the appropriateness or otherwise of any techniques described.

Library of Congress Cataloging-in-Publication Data

Author Name: Nosiri, Chizoma

Title: Self Epiphany Esteem & Confidence: Discover Your Purpose & Live Empowered / Dr. Chizoma Nosiri.

Description: Maryland : Irison, LLC (Irison Books & Publications)., [2020]

International Standard Book Number (ISBN) : 978-0-578-63058-8

Subjects: Self Help / Self Esteem / Confidence / Spirituality / God / Religion / Jesus Christ / Goal-Setting / Life / General.

Self-Paced Coaching Videos

This workbook and the **Self Epiphany Esteem & Confidence** book has online self-paced coaching videos which allows readers to further explore the concepts within the book in a more video content-rich delivery beyond the normal text audio format. In addition, the self-paced videos coaches readers through enhancing the book's concepts and activities in a dynamic layout to propel proactivity and promote further spiritual and mental growth. Find out more about the online self-paced coaching videos for **Self Epiphany Esteem & Confidence** by going to www.irisonbp.com.

Dedication

This book is dedicated to those who have wondered and searched to discover themselves and their capabilities. It is in the self that you find God. God meets you where you are, represents you to a reflection of your inherent Greatness, and propels you to a fulfillment of your many potentials. Always remember that empowerment lies within you as a God-given right.

CONTENTS

Your Journal Notes: Questions & Answers — viii

STEP I: Prepare to Embrace The Ultimate Epiphany — 1
CHAPTER I: Understand How to Recognize an Epiphany

Q&A Self-Reflection Questionnaire: Mental Epiphany — 3

Q&A Self-Reflection Questionnaire: Spiritual Epiphany — 5

Q&A Self-Reflection Questionnaire: Ultimate Epiphany — 9

STEP II: Represent Yourself — 17
CHAPTER II: Understand Yourself without the Worldly/Temporal Self Concept

Q&A Self-Reflection Questionnaire: Your "Self" — 19

Q&A Self-Reflection Questionnaire: Your Temporal Self — 23

Q&A Self-Reflection Questionnaire: Your Spiritual Self — 27

STEP III: Esteem Yourself — 35
CHAPTER III: "Esteem" Defined

Q&A Self-Reflection Questionnaire: Your Temporal Esteem — 37

Q&A Self-Reflection Questionnaire: Your Ego — 43

ACTIVITY- Remove the Ego — 47

Q&A Self-Reflection Questionnaire: Your Spiritual Esteem — 49

Q&A Self-Reflection Questionnaire: Healthy Self Esteem — 55

ACTIVITY – Healthy Self Esteem Today — 59

STEP IV: Discover Your Purpose   61
CHAPTER IV: Understanding the Role of Jesus Christ & Your Connection to Him

Q&A Self-Reflection Questionnaire: Temporal Epiphany   63

Q&A Self-Reflection Questionnaire: Jesus Christ, the "Sun" of God: Spiritual Epiphany   73

ACTIVITY – Scripture Search: Jesus Christ As Your Guide   77

STEP V: Live Empowered   79
CHAPTER V: Living Your Potential as the "Sun" of God

Q&A Self-Reflection Questionnaire: You, the "Sun" of God: Spiritual Epiphany   81

ACTIVITY – Greatness Word Cloud   89

Q&A Self-Reflection Questionnaire: Living as the "Sun" of God   91

ACTIVITY - Living As the "Sun" of God: Through Godly Greatness Thoughts   95

Q&A Awakening & Recognition of Your Unchangeable Greatness   97

ACTIVITY – Your Gifts   103

ACTIVITY – Your Talents   105

ACTIVITY – Your Skills   107

Q&A Activate Your Potential & Purpose Through Your GTS   109

About the Author   113

Your Journal Notes: Questions & Answers

Let thine heart retain my words: keep my commandments, and live. Get wisdom, get understanding: forget it not; neither decline from the words of my mouth. Forsake her not, and she shall preserve thee: love her, and she shall keep thee. Wisdom is the principal thing; therefore get wisdom: and with all thy getting get understanding. - Proverbs 4: 4-7

But be ye doers of the word, and not hearers only, deceiving your own selves. For if any be a hearer of the word, and not a doer, he is like unto a man beholding his natural face in a glass: For he beholdeth himself, and goeth his way, and straightway forgetteth what manner of man he was. But whoso looketh into the perfect law of liberty, and continueth therein, he being not a forgetful hearer, but a doer of the work, this man shall be blessed in his deed. -James 1: 22-25

As you read the **Self Epiphany Esteem & Confidence** book (which can be purchased online), you will be asked to answer questions pertaining to what you are feeling and learning. When you see the question sign **Q&A.** as you read, it is best to pause and reflect on the question that you are being asked. You can then answer the question in detail using this Self Epiphany Esteem & Confidence Workbook.

Step I
Prepare to Embrace the Ultimate Epiphany

CHAPTER I

A Mental Epiphany

Q&A. Mental Epiphany:

Have you ever experienced a mental epiphany? If yes, how did receiving a mental epiphany make you feel? Explain what happened in detail. If no, find someone who has and ask them to explain to you want happened to them and write it in details.

A Spiritual Epiphany

Q&A. Spiritual Epiphany:

Have you ever experienced a spiritual epiphany?

If yes, explain what happened in detail. If no, find someone who has and ask them to explain to you their spiritual epiphany experience.

How did receiving a spiritual epiphany make you feel?

The Ultimate Epiphany: Mind & Spirit

Q&A. Ultimate Epiphany:

Whether you have ever experienced an ultimate epiphany or not, what do you hope it will feel like for you?

___
___
___
___
___
___
___
___
___
___
___
___
___
___
___
___
___
___
___
___
___

If you have not Ultimate Epiphany how do you think it would change your mental perspective? If you have experienced an Ultimate Epiphany how did it change your mental perspective?

If you have not experienced an Ultimate Epiphany how do you think it would change your spiritual core? If you have experienced an Ultimate Epiphany how did it change your spiritual core?

Are you open to receiving an epiphany regardless of the "newness" (overwhelming outcome of the mental and/or spiritual knowledge/wisdom, or a call to action for you to change behaviors/mindset) it brings? Explain in detail why you feel this way.

Step II

Represent Yourself

CHAPTER II

Self "Defined

Q&A. Your "Self":

How do you define "self"?

How do you understand your thoughts of "self" in relationship to who you are?

The Temporal Self

Q&A. Your Temporal Self:

Are you aware when your temporal self is making the decisions in your life?

How do you control your temporal self?

The Spiritual Self

Q&A. Your Spiritual Self:

Do you focus on your spiritual "self" or the temporal "self", and why?

Which "self" do you think is more important to pay attention to and why should that "self" be more relevant?

How do you control your spiritual self?

In what ways can you be more in tune with your spiritual self and gain more control of focusing on living with your spiritual self as your centering of whole self (allowing your spiritual self to be more dominant than your temporal self)?

Step III

Esteem Yourself

CHAPTER III

"Esteem" Defined

Q&A. Your Temporal Esteem:

How have you been living with your temporal esteem as your main guide to happiness?

Are you aware when your temporal esteem is making the decisions in your life?

How can you control your temporal esteem or limit your temporal esteem?

The Ego

Q&A. Your Ego:

How has your ego prevented you from living the joyful life you deserve?

How can you start to limit your ego and embrace a God-centered perspective of yourself?

ACTIVITY- Remove the Ego

List ten (10) things you will start to do today and keep doing to lessen the attachment to your ego and grow close to a pureness with positive spiritual strength.

1. _____

2. _____

3. _____

4. _____

5. _____

6. _____

7. _____

8. _____

9. _____

10._____

The Spiritual Esteem

Q&A. Your Spiritual Esteem:

Have you been living with your spiritual esteem as your main guide to joy? If not, why? Explain in detail.

Are you aware when your spiritual esteem is making the decisions in your life?

How can you embrace and cultivate your spiritual esteem? What will be the best ways that you can harness your spiritual esteem as your guide?

Healthy Self "Esteem"

Q&A. Healthy Self Esteem:

Based on what you have read so far, do you think that you have Healthy Self Esteem?

_____

How do you apply healthy self esteem in your life?

_____
_____
_____
_____
_____
_____
_____
_____
_____
_____
_____
_____
_____
_____
_____
_____

What does healthy self esteem look like in your life?

ACTIVITY - Healthy Self Esteem Today

Each day do something small to show how much you love and care for yourself. (e.g. watch your favorite movie, chat with a dear friend about your day, cook your favorite meal, take a long bubble bath, make a healthy habit a daily consistent, laugh out loud, count your blessings, etc.)

List some of the activities you complete to showcase your progress:

Activity: _____

Activity: _____

Activity: _____

Activity: _____

Activity: _____

Activity: _____

Activity: _____

Activity: _____

Step IV

Discover Your Purpose

CHAPTER IV

Understanding the Role of Jesus Christ & Your Connection to Him

Q&A. Temporal Epiphany:

Based on what you have read about the birth of Jesus, how do you feel society looked at his family status and place of birth?

How was society's assessment of Jesus' birth family status and birth place the wrong interpretation?

How do you feel you have been treated based on society's assessment and social setup of today?

How will you start to see yourself from today forward?

Today, how can you apply a positive revolutionary and innovative perspective in how you see yourself?

Jesus *Christ,* the "Sun" of God

Spiritual Epiphany: Connection & Transformation

The Light from Within

Q&A. Jesus Christ, the "Sun" of God: Spiritual Epiphany:

Based on what you have read about the connection and transformation, how do you see yourself in the world today?

_____

_____

_____

_____

_____

_____

_____

_____

_____

_____

_____

_____

_____

_____

_____

_____

_____

_____

_____

_____

How can you apply the connection and transformation to living your daily life today?

ACTIVITY – Scripture Search: Jesus Christ As Your Guide

Search the New Testament of the Bible and make notes of other examples and ways that Jesus Christ changed the status quo of society, shared love for all, embraced individual uniqueness, and esteemed himself.

Example 1: _____

Example 2: _____

Example 3: _____

Example 4: _____

Example 5: _____

Example 6: _____

Example 7: _____

Example 8: _____

Example 9: _____

Example 10:_____

Step V

Live

Empowered

CHAPTER V

Step 5: Living Your Potential as the "Sun" of God

Q&A. You, the "Sun" of God: Spiritual Epiphany:
How do you believe JesusChrist and God see you?

How do you feel that you have been treated by social constructs, based on the message Jesus shares with you about your spiritual connection to Him and God? Explain in detail.

How does recognizing your Greatness make you feel?

How can you apply the connection and transformation to living your daily life today?

ACTIVITY – Greatness Word Cloud

As the Sun, you shine through the clouds and everything you touch is impacted with love, warmth and positivity. Draw a large cloud and in the cloud make a list of positive words that describe your Greatness and how God and Jesus Christ see you.

Q&A. Living as the "Sun" of God:

What does "self" love mean to you?

What does living as the "Sun" of God mean to you?

ACTIVITY - Living As the "Sun" of God: Through Godly Greatness Thoughts

I will always remember that I am:

_____
_____
_____
_____
_____

I will start living my life in a way that:

_____
_____
_____
_____
_____

I promise to live each day with:

_____
_____
_____
_____
_____

Q&A. Awakening & Recognition of Your Unchangeable Greatness

How have you been awakened from this book?

How will you express this great message that Jesus Christ has delivered to you as you live your life?

How will you share your Greatness and reach your potential?

ACTIVITY – Embrace Your GTS – Your Gifts

Make a list of your Gifts (e.g. intuition, discernment, empathy, etc.):

My Gift: _____

My Gift: _____

My Gift: _____

My Gift: _____

My Gift: _____

My Gift: _____

My Gift: _____

My Gift: _____

My Gift: _____

My Gift: _____

ACTIVITY – Embrace Your GTS – Your Talents

Make a list of your Talents (expert in playing an instrument, singing, drawing, etc.):

My Talent: _____

My Talent: _____

My Talent: _____

My Talent: _____

My Talent: _____

My Talent: _____

My Talent: _____

My Talent: _____

My Talent: _____

My Talent: _____

ACTIVITY – Embrace Your GTS – Your Skills

Make a list of your Skills (computer skills, crafting, organizational skills, etc.):

My Skills: _____

My Skills: _____

My Skills: _____

My Skills: _____

My Skills: _____

My Skills: _____

My Skills: _____

My Skills: _____

My Skills: _____

My Skills: _____

Q&A. Activate Your Potential & Purpose Through Your GTS

How will you start honing your Greatness (Gifts, Talents, Skills) attributes so you can live and shine as the Sun of God, self-actualize, and reach your potential?

_____
_____
_____
_____
_____
_____
_____
_____
_____
_____
_____
_____
_____
_____
_____
_____
_____
_____
_____
_____
_____
_____
_____
_____

"Your Greatness is truth within your existence. Healthy self esteem and confidence abound in lifestyle." - Dr. Chizoma Nosiri

About the Author

Dr. Chizoma C. Nosiri is a self esteem guru, confidence expert, and world renowned positive communication theorist, public speaking lecturer, culture and organizational change consultant. Her research has impacted the disciplines of intrapersonal and interpersonal communication, gender, consumerism, international communication, organizational communication, and conflict mediation and resolution. As a change agent, Dr. Nosiri works with corporations, organizations, and individuals to change their communication processes. She has been featured on several radio and television shows as a communication and confidence guru.

Dr. Nosiri founded NOSIRI Empowerment Center (www.nosiri.com) to build individuals, organizations and corporations. NOSIRI is the only facilitator of the positive communication and applied empowerment coaching approach created by Dr. Nosiri, which produces immediate, impactful long-lasting success. NOSIRI is noted as the paramount training organization that unites core areas of personal and professional development into one, combining self esteem, confidence, public speaking classes, leaderships, and Dr. Nosiri's positive communication and applied empowerment coaching and training. Dr. Nosiri books, lectures and seminars, and sessions are life-changing.

Other books by Dr. Nosiri includes, "The Global Woman's Impact on E-Commerce: Confidence and Communication Clashes with Western Corporations".

Dr. Nosiri believes that, "When you change your mindset, you change your life."

www.ingramcontent.com/pod-product-compliance
Lightning Source LLC
Chambersburg PA
CBHW040907020526
44114CB00038B/85